THE OFFICIAL
ENGLAND

ANNUAL 2020

Written by Andy Greeves
Designed by Chris Dalrymple

D1337210

A Grange Publication

© 2019. Published by Grange Communications Ltd.,
Edinburgh, under licence from The Football Association.

Printed in the EU.

ISBN 978-1-913034-18-4

CONTENTS

WELCOME TO THE OFFICIAL ENGLAND ANNUAL 2020

It's a hugely exciting and proud time to be an England supporter, with both the Three Lions and the Lionesses enjoying multiple successes and star players.

2019 saw the men's senior side finish third at the inaugural UEFA Nations League finals while the Lionesses triumphed in the SheBelieves Cup and reached the semi-final of the FIFA Women's World Cup. Summer 2020 will see Wembley Stadium host seven UEFA EURO 2020 matches, including both semi-finals and the final on July 12. Here's hoping Gareth Southgate's Three Lions will be at the thick of the action as the tournament celebrates its 60th anniversary.

We'll take a look back at the memorable matches our teams have been involved in during recent times, and explore the history of the Three Lions, plus their greatest moments. The players that make up the England's senior men's and women's squads are profiled, and we introduce some of The FA's SuperKicks challenges. With quizzes and games to test the knowledge of even the most diehard England supporter, there's plenty to keep fans young and old happily entertained.

COME ON ENGLAND

#ThreeLions #Lionesses

PRIDE OF THE NATION

Almost 150 years on from playing in world football's first-ever full international, The Three Lions remain at the forefront of the global game, boasting a rich history and a bright future...

Early Days

Between 1870 and 1872, the Football Association – founded in 1863 – organised a series of matches between teams representing England and Scotland. The first of those fixtures – which aren't recognised by FIFA as full internationals as the Scotland side consisted only of London-based, Scottish players - took place at The Oval in London on March 5, 1870. The first 'official' match between the two sides, indeed the first full international in world football history, took place at Hamilton Crescent in Partick on November 30, 1872 and ended in a goalless draw.

For almost the first 40 years, the England national team played exclusively against Scotland, Wales and Ireland. The inaugural British Home Championships, involving all four nations, was first held during the 1883/84 season. The Three Lions claimed the first of their record 54 successes in the tournament in 1886, sharing the trophy with Scotland that year, before enjoying their first outright win in 1888. Apart from the years during the two World Wars and during the 1980/81 season, the competition took place every year through until 1984.

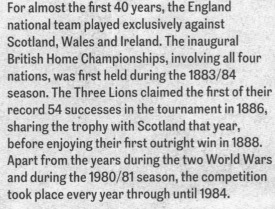

England became a member of Fédération Internationale de Football Association (FIFA) in 1905. Three years later, they faced their first opponents from outside of the United Kingdom and Ireland as they embarked on a tour of central Europe, taking on Austria, Hungary and Bohemia.

On April 12 1924, England staged their first match at Wembley Stadium, which opened the previous year. The game against Scotland ended in a 1-1 draw. Over the next 27 years, Wembley was only used when the Three Lions faced the Scots until a match-up with Argentina in May 1951. Thereafter, the ground was increasingly used by the national team, with only ten England 'home' games between 1951 and 1999 played away from Wembley.

In 1950 England competed in the FIFA World Cup for the first time but were eliminated at the group stage. Four years later, the Three Lions got to the quarter-finals of the competition where they bowed out to reigning world champions Uruguay.

United Kingdom's most-watched televised event of all-time. Helmut Haller gave the West Germans a 12th minute lead in the showpiece fixture, but a Geoff Hurst header saw England level six minutes later. Martin Peters put the Three Lions in front with just 13 minutes of the game remaining but Wolfgang Weber's effort with just seconds left forced extra-time.

In the added period of 30 minutes, Hurst scored twice to complete his hat-trick and a 4-2 victory for England. Captain Bobby Moore collected the Jules Rimet trophy from Queen Elizabeth II and was later held aloft on the shoulders of teammates Hurst and Ray Wilson to create a series of iconic photographs.

England entered the UEFA European Championships for the first time in 1968, finishing third at the tournament (further details on the Three Lions' exploits at the European Championships can be found on pages 52 to 55). Two years later, their defence of the World Cup ended at the quarter-final stage of the tournament in Mexico as they were beaten 3-2 by West Germany.

Failure to qualify for the 1974 FIFA World Cup resulted in the dismissal of Ramsey while the Three Lions also missed out on the 1978 tournament in Argentina. They returned to the competition in 1982 but were eliminated in the second group stage despite never losing a game in Spain. England striker Gary Lineker was the top goal scorer at the 1986 FIFA World Cup as Sir Bobby Robson's side reached the quarter-final of the competition. Two goals from Diego Maradona – one, a hugely controversial effort that has since been dubbed the 'Hand of God', the second, a brilliant solo effort described as the 'Goal of the Century' – separated the sides. Lineker got a late consolation for Robson's team.

Champions of the World

England were knocked out of the 1958 FIFA World Cup at the group stage and made the quarter-finals in 1962 before staging the tournament for the first time in 1966. After a goalless draw with Uruguay in the opening fixture of the 16-team competition, Sir Alf Ramsey's men topped Group 1, beating Mexico and France. They then overcame Argentina and Portugal in the quarter-finals and semi-finals respectively.

The final against West Germany was held at Wembley Stadium on July 30 1966. In addition to a crowd of 96,924 inside the 'Home of Football', a peak British television audience of 32.3 million tuned into the match – making the match the

Nine minutes into extra-time, Paul Gascoigne was booked for a sliding challenge on Thomas Berthold. Having picked up his second yellow card of the knockout phase, Gazza knew he would miss the final should England get there. Cue tears. "My bottom lip was like a helicopter pad," the talismanic midfielder once reflected on the incident. Alas, Sir Bobby Robson's men were beaten 4-3 in the ensuing penalty shootout and lost 2-1 to hosts Italy in the third-place play-off match three days later.

England were involved in some truly memorable tournament matches in the second half of the 1990s. Terry Venables' side reached the semi-final of UEFA Euro 1996, which included group stage victories over Scotland and the Netherlands. The Three Lions were knocked out of the 1998 FIFA World Cup at the round of 16 stage by Argentina but only after an epic clash in Saint-Étienne. Michael Owen scored an incredible solo goal for Glenn Hoddle's team as the match finished 2-2 after extra-time. Unfortunately, the Three Lions were beaten in a penalty shootout.

On October 7, 2000, Germany beat England 1-0 in the last-ever match at the original Wembley Stadium – which was subsequently demolished and replaced by a brand-new stadium which opened in 2007. In the corresponding 2002 FIFA World Cup qualifying match, the Three Lions got their revenge, winning 5-1 in Munich on September 1, 2001. It was England's biggest win since a 6-0 triumph over Luxembourg in 1999 and only the third time in which Germany had lost by four or more goals at that stage of their history.

Gazza's Tears

As they had at UEFA Euro 1988, England faced the Republic of Ireland in their opening group fixture at the 1990 FIFA World Cup in Italy. Kevin Sheedy's second-half equaliser for the Boys in Green cancelled out Gary Lineker's effort in the first period as the match ended in a 1-1 draw. After a goalless encounter with the Netherlands in their second game, England topped their group with a 1-0 victory over Egypt in Cagliari on June 21, 1990.

David Platt's winner in the last-minute of extra-time saw the Three Lions to a 1-0 victory over Belgium in the round of 16. They also beat Cameroon 3-2 in Naples in a match in which Lineker netted twice from the penalty spot. An epic semi-final clash with West Germany took place at the Stadio delle Alpi in Turin on July 4, 1990. Andreas Brehme opened the scoring before Lineker's equaliser ten minutes from time saw a third England World Cup match in a row require an additional period of 30 minutes to be added.

The 21st Century

In 2001, Sven-Göran Eriksson became the first non-English manager of the Three Lions. The Swede guided his team to the quarter-finals of the 2002 and 2006 FIFA World Cups as well as UEFA Euro 2004 as the nation rose to number four in the world rankings. The team around that period, which contained the likes of David Beckham, Michael Owen, Wayne Rooney, Steven Gerrard and Frank Lampard was dubbed the 'Golden Generation' by sections of the British media.

On June 1 2007, England played their first match at the 'new' Wembley Stadium, drawing 1-1 with Brazil in front of a crowd of 88,745. Having missed out on qualification for UEFA Euro 2008, the Three Lions reached the last 16 of the FIFA World Cup in South Africa in 2010, where they were beaten 4-1 by Germany. Seven points from three matches saw England top Group D at UEFA Euro 2012 but penalty shootout agony ensued once again as Roy Hodgson's side lost 4-2 on spot-kicks to Italy after a goalless quarter-final tie in Kiev on June 24, 2012.

The 2014 FIFA World Cup saw England finished bottom of a tricky group containing Italy, Uruguay and Costa Rica, while they ended up on the wrong end of an upset at UEFA Euro 2016, going down to a 2-1 defeat to Iceland in the round of 16.

The disappointment of previous tournaments was largely forgotten in 2018 as Gareth Southgate's Three Lions reached the semi-final of the FIFA World Cup in Russia. Harry Kane won the Golden

Boot with six goals in as many matches, including a hat-trick in a 6-1 win over Panama in Nizhny Novgorod on June 24 2018. The round of 16 match against Colombia in Moscow on July 3 2018 was notable as England enjoyed their first-ever World Cup penalty shootout success at the fourth attempt. After a 1-1 draw after extra-time, Eric Dier struck home the winning spot-kick in a 4-3 success.

Kieran Trippier gave England a fifth-minute lead against Croatia in the semi-final of the tournament but an equaliser from Ivan Perišić and an extra-time winner from Mario Mandžukić saw the Three Lions' hopes of making it to their first World Cup Final since 1966 dashed.

England's excellent performances in 2018 continued with victories over Spain and Croatia in the UEFA Nations League, as Southgate's side made the finals of the tournament, where they finished third in Portugal in 2019.

The future looks bright for England at senior men's level as it does throughout the age group ranks. In 2017, the Three Lions celebrated World Cup triumphs at Under-17 and Under-20 level.

UEFA NATIONS LEAGUE REVIEW 2018/19

UEFA NATIONS LEAGUE™

England produced some excellent performances in the newly-formed UEFA Nations League...

UEFA Nations League A Group 4

England's UEFA Nations League campaign got underway with a home match against Spain on September 8, 2018. Marcus Rashford put the Three Lions ahead after 11 minutes but Saúl Ñíguez equalised two minutes later. A Rodrigo Moreno strike 13 minutes from the break ultimately proved to be the visitors' winner.

Gareth Southgate's side travelled to Croatia for their second group match the following month when England hit the woodwork twice in a goalless draw. Three days later, they claimed an impressive 3-2 victory in Spain. Raheem Sterling scored his first international goal in three years to put the Three Lions one-up after 16 minutes.

Rashford got on the end of a magnificent through-ball from Kane to double their advantage on 29 minutes while Sterling got his second of the night seven minutes before half-time. Paco Alcácer and Sergio Ramos got goals for Spain in the second-half but England held on for an important win in Seville.

Spain's 3-2 defeat in Zagreb on November 15, 2018 meant England and Croatia met at Wembley Stadium three days later knowing the winning team would top Group 4 and make it to the 2019 UEFA

Nations League Finals. After a goalless first-half, the visitors took a 57th minute lead through Andrej Kramarić. The Three Lions equalised with 12 minutes remaining as Jesse Lingard helped a toe-poke from Kane across the Croatian goal line. Seven minutes later, Kane got on the end of a free-kick from Ben Chilwell to bag his 20th international goal and send England through to the finals in Portugal.

UEFA Nations League A Group 4 – Final Table

Pos		P	W	D	L	GF	GA	GD	PTS
1	ENGLAND	4	2	1	1	6	5	1	7
2	SPAIN	4	2	0	2	12	7	5	6
3	CROATIA	4	1	1	2	4	10	6	4

2019 UEFA Nations League Finals

England took on the Netherlands in their UEFA Nations League semi-final, staged in Guimarães, Portugal on June 6 2019. The Three Lions went ahead after 29 minutes through a Rashford penalty.

Matthijs de Ligt equalised with 17 minutes of the game remaining, heading in from a corner to force extra-time. In the added period of 30 minutes, an own-goal from Kyle Walker and a further strike from Quincy Promes saw the Dutch run out as 3-1 winners.

Three days later, Southgate's side faced Switzerland in the tournament's third-place play-off. Kane hit the Swiss crossbar in the opening few minutes of the match, while Sterling also struck the woodwork during a game dominated by England. Callum Wilson had an 83rd-minute 'goal' disallowed before the match eventually had to be settled by a penalty shootout. Harry Maguire, Ross Barkley, Jadon Sancho, Sterling, goalkeeper Pickford and Dier all dispatched their spot-kicks before Pickford saved from Josip Drmić to secure a 6-5 shootout victory for England.

A FESTIVAL OF FOOTBALL

To mark the 60th anniversary of the European Championships, UEFA Euro 2020 (June 12 to July 12, 2020) matches will be staged in 12 cities across the continent, with the semi-finals and final taking place at Wembley Stadium.

History

The idea for a pan-European football tournament was first mooted by the French Football Federation's Secretary General Henri Delaunay in 1927. However, it wasn't until 1958 – three years after Delaunay's death – that the European Championship finally came into existence.

The first Championship took place in France in 1960, with the Soviet Union beating Yugoslavia 2-1 in the final. The host nation and Czechoslovakia also competed in the four-team competition, while England, the Netherlands, West Germany and Italy were among nations who didn't enter the qualifying tournament.

After the 1964 and 1968 Championships – the latter which saw the Three Lions' first foray into competition - the tournament was expanded to eight teams ahead of the 1980 edition. UEFA Euro 1996, which was hosted in England, featured 16 nations competing for the first-time. Then in 2016, 24 countries took part.

Year	Hosts	Winners
1960	France	Soviet Union
1964	Spain	Spain
1968	Italy	Italy
1972	Belgium	West Germany
1976	Yugoslavia	Czechslovakia
1980	Italy	West Germany
1984	France	France
1988	West Germany	Netherlands
1992	Sweden	Denmark
1996	England	Germany
2000	Belgium/Netherlands	France
2004	Portugal	Greece
2008	Austria/Switzerland	Spain
2012	Poland/Ukraine	Spain
2016	France	Portugal

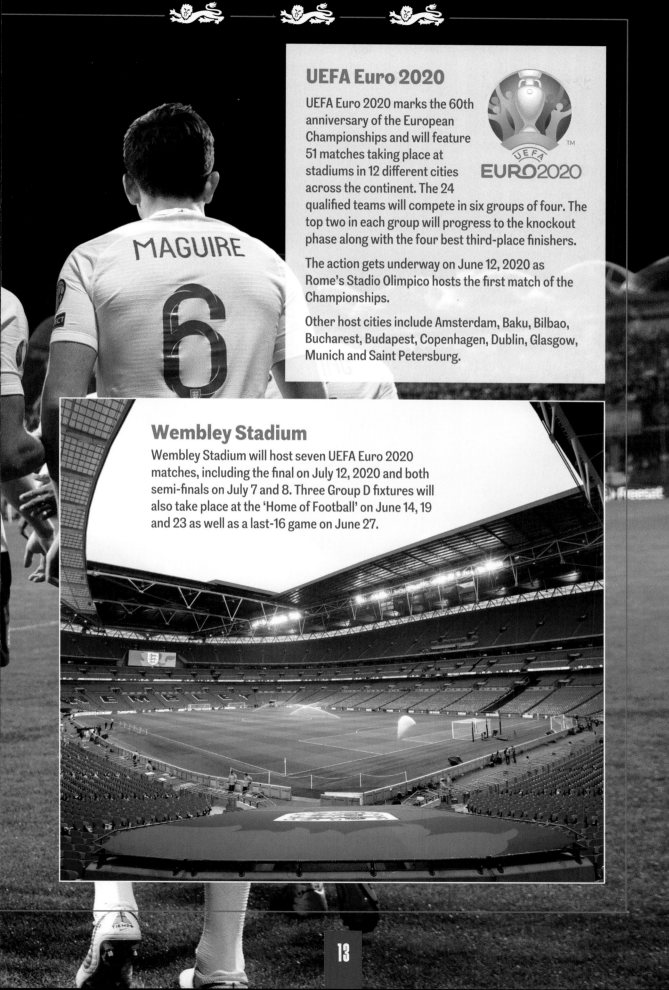

UEFA Euro 2020

UEFA Euro 2020 marks the 60th anniversary of the European Championships and will feature 51 matches taking place at stadiums in 12 different cities across the continent. The 24 qualified teams will compete in six groups of four. The top two in each group will progress to the knockout phase along with the four best third-place finishers.

The action gets underway on June 12, 2020 as Rome's Stadio Olimpico hosts the first match of the Championships.

Other host cities include Amsterdam, Baku, Bilbao, Bucharest, Budapest, Copenhagen, Dublin, Glasgow, Munich and Saint Petersburg.

Wembley Stadium

Wembley Stadium will host seven UEFA Euro 2020 matches, including the final on July 12, 2020 and both semi-finals on July 7 and 8. Three Group D fixtures will also take place at the 'Home of Football' on June 14, 19 and 23 as well as a last-16 game on June 27.

GARETH SOUTHGATE

MANAGER PROFILE

FULL NAME:
GARETH SOUTHGATE

DATE OF BIRTH:
SEPTEMBER 3, 1970

PLACE OF BIRTH:
WATFORD

ENGLAND MEN'S SENIOR MANAGER:
SINCE SEPTEMBER 2016

Gareth Southgate spent all but one of his 16 seasons as a professional footballer playing in the top division of English league football. He rose through the ranks at Crystal Palace to make his senior debut for the Eagles in a League Cup tie against Southend United in October 1990 before making his league debut at Liverpool in April 1991.

Southgate played in various positions at Palace, including right-back and central midfield, and was appointed club Captain at the age of 23. He skippered them during their title-winning season in the old First Division in 1993-94. After making 191 appearances and scoring 22 goals, he departed the south London club for Aston Villa in the summer of 1995.

Southgate was converted into a centre-back during his time with the Villans, for whom he won the League Cup in 1995/96. After featuring in a total of 243 games for the club, netting eight times, he was on the move again in the summer of 2001, signing for fellow Premier League outfit Middlesbrough. He formed a fine central defensive partnership with the late Ugo Ehiogu during his time at the Riverside Stadium and captained Boro to their first – and, to date, only – major trophy success as they won the League Cup in 2004.

During his playing career, Southgate won 57 caps for England and scored twice against Luxembourg in October 1998 and South Africa in May 2003. He made his debut for the Three Lions as a substitute in a 1-1 draw with Portugal at Wembley Stadium in December 1995 while his first start came in a 1-0 victory over Bulgaria three months later. The defender was selected in Terry Venables' 22-man squad for UEFA Euro 1996 and started in all five of England's matches at the tournament.

Southgate also represented England at the 1998 and 2002 FIFA World Cups, as well as UEFA Euro 2000. Fittingly for a former Aston Villa player, his 50th cap for the Three Lions came in a 1-1 draw with Portugal at Villa Park in September 2002 while his final appearance for his country came in a 1-0 defeat to Sweden in Gothenburg in March 2004. He is Aston Villa's most capped England player, having played 42 of his 57 internationals whilst with the Villans. Southgate retired from playing at the end of the 2005-06 season, with his last match as a professional coming in Middlesbrough's 4-0 defeat to Sevilla in the 2006 UEFA Cup Final.

Soon after hanging up his boots, Southgate was handed the opportunity to become manager of Middlesbrough as a replacement for Steve McClaren, who had taken the top job with England. He departed the Riverside Stadium in October 2009, with

Boro having dropped from the Premier League to the Championship by this stage.

He became England's U21 manager in August 2013 and achieved qualification to the 2015 UEFA U21 EURO Finals during his reign. He worked with a number of players at that level who have now become regulars in the Three Lions' senior squad including John Stones, Jordan Pickford, Raheem Sterling, Marcus Rashford, Harry Kane, Eric Dier and Jesse Lingard.

Following Sam Allardyce's departure, Southgate was put in temporary charge of the England senior team in September 2016. His first match was a 2-0 win over Malta at Wembley Stadium a month later. His side achieved a win over Scotland and draws with Slovenia and Spain during his interim spell as manager, before Southgate was appointed on a permanent basis in November 2016.

With Southgate at the helm, England reached the semi-finals of the 2018 FIFA World Cup, which included the Three Lions' first-ever penalty shootout success at the tournament against Colombia in the round of 16. There were also victories against Tunisia, Panama and Sweden before the Three Lions were beaten 2-1 after extra-time in their last-four tie against Croatia.

There was further success for Southgate's England in 2018, as they topped their UEFA Nations League group to make it through to the inaugural finals of the competition. An extra-time defeat to the Netherlands followed by a 6-5 penalty shootout success over Switzerland in Portugal in 2019 saw the Three Lions finish third at a major tournament for the first time since UEFA Euro 1968.

MEN'S SENIOR TEAM PROFILES

(H) Home (A) Away (N) Neutral Venue

JORDAN PICKFORD

JACK BUTLAND

TOM HEATON

KYLE WALKER

JOHN STONES

DANNY ROSE

HARRY MAGUIRE

MICHAEL KEANE

BEN CHILWELL

JOE GOMEZ

TRENT ALEXANDER-ARNOLD

JORDAN HENDERSON

ERIC DIER

DELE

ROSS BARKLEY

JESSE LINGARD

FABIAN DELPH

DECLAN RICE

RUBEN LOFTUS-CHEEK

HARRY KANE

MARCUS RASHFORD

JADON SANCHO

CALLUM WILSON

RAHEEM STERLING

CALLUM HUDSON-ODOI

JORDAN PICKFORD

Position: Goalkeeper **Date of Birth:** March 7, 1994
Place of Birth: Washington **Current Club:** Everton
England Debut: November 10, 2017 v Germany (H)

Prior to making his senior international debut in a goalless draw following with Germany at Wembley Stadium in 2017, Jordan Pickford had played for England at all levels between U16 up to and including U21. The 6'1" goalkeeper started all seven matches for the Three Lions at the 2018 FIFA World Cup. In the round of 16 clash with Colombia at the tournament, he produced an incredible one-handed stop from a Carlos Bacca spot-kick to help England to their first-ever World Cup penalty shootout success at the fourth attempt. After a goalless draw following extra-time in the UEFA Nations League Finals third-place play-off against Switzerland in 2019, he produced more heroics, saving a Josip Drmić spot-kick. He also became the first England goalkeeper to take (and score) a penalty in a competitive shootout as the Three Lions won 6-5.

JACK BUTLAND

Position: Goalkeeper **Date of Birth:** March 10, 1993
Place of Birth: Bristol **Current Club:** Stoke City
England Debut: August 15, 2012 v Italy (N)

Jack Butland's first involvement with the England senior team came when he was included in the squad for UEFA Euro 2012. He became the Three Lions' youngest-ever goalkeeper when he made his international debut against Italy in Bern in August 2012 at the age of 19 years and 158 days. His first competitive appearance came in a 3-0 UEFA Euro 2016 qualifying victory in Lithuania in October 2015. He suffered a fractured ankle in a match against Germany in March 2016 which saw him ruled out for that year's European Championships but he was named in Gareth Southgate's 23-man squad for the FIFA World Cup two years later.

TOM HEATON

Position: Goalkeeper **Date of Birth:** April 15, 1986
Place of Birth: Chester **Current Club:** Aston Villa
England Debut: May 27, 2016 v Australia (H)

Like Pickford and Butland, Tom Heaton is another goalkeeper that has been capped at various youth and development levels for England, including U16, U17, U18, U19 and U21. His senior debut came as an 87th-minute substitute for Fraser Forster in a friendly match against Australia at Sunderland AFC's Stadium of Light in May 2016, while his first international start came in a 3-2 to France at the Stade de France in Saint-Denis in June 2017.

KYLE WALKER

Position: Defender **Date of Birth:** May 28, 1990
Place of Birth: Sheffield **Current Club:** Manchester City
England Debut: November 12, 2011 v Spain (H)

In February 2009, Kyle Walker was called up to the England U19 squad for the first time before he had even made a league appearance for his first professional club, Sheffield United. A few years later, he was named in the Team of the Tournament following his performances for the U21s at the 2011 UEFA U-21 Championships in Denmark. Since making his senior debut against Spain in November 2011, the right-sided defender has become a regular feature in the Three Lions squad and featured at both UEFA Euro 2016 and the 2018 FIFA World Cup.

JOHN STONES

Position: Defender **Date of Birth:** May 28, 1994
Place of Birth: Barnsley **Current Club:** Manchester City
England Debut: May 30, 2014 v Peru (H)

John Stones played in all seven of England's matches at the 2018 FIFA World Cup, where he scored his first international goals, by bagging a brace in a 6-1 win over Panama at the tournament. Since making his debut against Peru in May 2014, the Manchester City defender was called up for UEFA Euro 2016 and the 2019 UEFA Nations League finals, where he started the semi-final match-up with the Netherlands. The Barnsley-born centre-back previously appeared for the Young Lions at U19, U20 and U21 level.

DANNY ROSE

Position: Defender **Date of Birth:** July 2, 1990
Place of Birth: Doncaster **Current Club:** Tottenham Hotspur
England Debut: March 26, 2016 v Germany (A)

In addition to appearances for England at U16, U17, U18 and U19 level, Danny Rose won 29 caps for the U21s between 2009 and 2013, scoring three times. His senior international debut came in a memorable 3-2 win for the Three Lions over Germany at the Olympiastadion in Berlin in March 2016. He played in three of England's four matches at UEFA Euro 2016 and featured in five games at the 2018 FIFA World Cup. He won his 25th cap in England's 1-0 victory over Switzerland in a friendly at Leicester City FC's King Power Stadium in September 2018.

HARRY MAGUIRE

Position: Defender **Date of Birth:** March 5, 1993
Place of Birth: Sheffield **Current Club:** Manchester United
England Debut: October 8, 2017 v Lithuania (A)

Harry Maguire was part of an England defence that kept clean sheets in his first five senior international appearances against Lithuania, Germany, Brazil, Netherlands and Costa Rica. The then-Leicester City centre-back was an important member of Gareth Southgate's squad for the 2018 FIFA World Cup, featuring in all seven games at the tournament. His first goal for the Three Lions came in the 2-0 win over Sweden in the quarter-final while he started in both matches at the 2019 UEFA Nations League finals.

MICHAEL KEANE

Position: Defender **Date of Birth:** January 11, 1993
Place of Birth: Stockport **Current Club:** Everton
England Debut: March 22, 2017 v Germany (A)

Michael Keane played for the Republic of Ireland's U17 and U19 teams before switching his international allegiance to England in 2012, for who he was capped at U19, U20 and U21 level. The defender made his senior debut in a 1-0 defeat to Germany in Dortmund in March 2017, while he also played in the 2-0 win over Lithuania at Wembley Stadium that same month. His first international goal came in an impressive 5-1 victory for the Three Lions away in Montenegro in a UEFA Euro 2020 qualifying match in March 2019.

BEN CHILWELL

Position: Defender **Date of Birth:** December 21, 1996
Place of Birth: Milton Keynes **Current Club:** Leicester City
England Debut: September 11, 2018 v Switzerland (H)

Along with Leicester City team-mate Demarai Gray, Ben Chilwell received his first senior England call-up for a friendly against Switzerland in September 2018. He made his first appearance for the Three Lions in that match, held at the Foxes' King Power Stadium. In doing so, he became the first player to debut for England at their home club ground since former Manchester United midfielder Paul Scholes came on as a second-half substitute for Teddy Sheringham against South Africa at Old Trafford in 1997. Chilwell started in England's UEFA Nations League finals clash against the Netherlands in June 2019.

JOE GOMEZ

Position: Defender **Date of Birth:** May 23, 1997
Place of Birth: London **Current Club:** Liverpool
England Debut: November 10, 2017 v Germany (H)

A product of Charlton Athletic's youth academy, Joe Gomez joined Liverpool in 2015 and won the UEFA Champions League with the Merseysiders in 2019. After featuring for England at U16, U17, U19 and U21 level, the defender made his senior international debut against Germany at Wembley Stadium in November 2017. His second appearance for the Three Lions came against Brazil a few days later. He was named Man of the Match in the goalless draw, as he helped nullify the attacking threat of Brazilian forwards such as Neymar, Gabriel Jesus and Philippe Coutinho.

TRENT ALEXANDER-ARNOLD

Position: Defender **Date of Birth:** October 7, 1998
Place of Birth: Liverpool **Current Club:** Liverpool
England Debut: June 7, 2018 v Costa Rica (H)

Liverpool-born right-back Trent Alexander-Arnold made his debut for his home city team against Tottenham Hotspur in the League Cup in October 2016. He quickly established himself as a regular for club and country, with his first England appearance coming in a 2-0 victory over Costa Rica in a game at Leeds United's Elland Road in June 2018. He was included in the squad for the 2018 FIFA World Cup and featured in one match at the tournament in the group stage clash with Belgium. His first goal for the Three Lions came in the 3-0 victory over the United States in November 2018.

JORDAN HENDERSON

Position: Midfielder **Date of Birth:** June 17, 1990
Place of Birth: Sunderland **Current Club:** Liverpool
England Debut: November 17, 2010 v France (H)

With over 50 caps for England, Jordan Henderson is one of the most experienced members of Gareth Southgate's squad. The Sunderland-born midfielder represented his country at the 2014 and 2018 FIFA World Cups, as well as UEFA Euro 2012 and 2016, having previously played for and captained the U21s. He also featured at U19 and U20 level. Since making his senior international debut in a 2-1 defeat to France at Wembley Stadium in November 2010, the midfielder has captained the Three Lions on a number of occasions.

ERIC DIER

Position: Midfielder **Date of Birth:** January 15, 1994
Place of Birth: Cheltenham **Current Club:** Tottenham Hotspur
England Debut: November 13, 2015 v Spain (A)

Eric Dier's successful spot-kick and subsequent celebration after sealing England's penalty shootout victory over Colombia was one of the enduring images of the Three Lions' memorable 2018 FIFA World Cup campaign. The versatile Tottenham Hotspur player, who is able to play in either defence or midfield, made his England debut against Spain in Alicante in November 2015. His first goal for the Three Lions was their winner in the 3-2 triumph over Germany in March 2016 while he also netted in the 1-1 draw with Russia at UEFA Euro 2016. His 40th England cap came in the UEFA Nations League third-place play-off against Switzerland in June 2019.

DELE

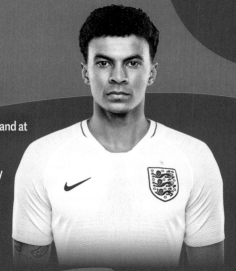

Position: Midfielder **Date of Birth:** April 11, 1996
Place of Birth: Milton Keynes **Current Club:** Tottenham Hotspur
England Debut: October 9, 2015 v Estonia (H)

A two-time PFA Young Player of the Year, Dele Alli appeared for England at U17, U18, U19 and U21 level before his elevation to the senior team in 2015. The attacking midfielder scored his first goal for the Three Lions on his fourth appearance, in a 2-0 win over France at Wembley Stadium in November 2015. He was also on target against Malta in 2016 before he netted at the World Cup for the first time in a 2-0 quarter-final victory Sweden in July 2018. As well as playing in five matches at that tournament, Dele featured in both of England's fixtures at the 2019 UEFA Nations League finals.

ROSS BARKLEY

Position: Midfielder **Date of Birth:** December 5, 1993
Place of Birth: Liverpool **Current Club:** Chelsea
England Debut: September 6, 2013 v Moldova (H)

Ross Barkley was named in England U17s Team of the Tournament that won the 2010 UEFA Under-17 Championships. The midfielder also featured at U16, U19, U20 and U21 level during the early years of his career, prior to making his senior debut in a 4-0 victory over Moldova at Wembley Stadium in September 2013. Goals are a regular feature of his game at club and international level, with his strikes for the Three Lions so far including a brace against Montenegro in a 5-1 away victory in March 2019.

JESSE LINGARD

Position: Midfielder **Date of Birth:** December 15, 1992
Place of Birth: Warrington **Current Club:** Manchester United
England Debut: October 8, 2016 v Malta (H)

Jesse Lingard has been a regular in Gareth Southgate's England squad since the manager's appointment in 2016. The midfielder made his debut in Southgate's first match in charge of the national team – a 2-0 victory against Malta in October 2016. The pair had previously worked together at U21 level, with ten of Lingard's eleven caps for the Young Lions coming under Southgate's management. Lingard scored his first goal for England in a 1-0 win over the Netherlands in Amsterdam in March 2018 while he also netted in the 6-1 triumph over Panama at the 2018 FIFA World Cup.

FABIAN DELPH

Position: Midfielder **Date of Birth:** November 21, 1989
Place of Birth: Bradford **Current Club:** Everton
England Debut: September 3, 2014 V Norway (H)

Fabian Delph began his international career representing England U19s for two matches in 2008. He then made four appearances for the U21s before making his senior debut in a 1-0 win over Norway in 2014. He featured in four games for the Three Lions at the 2018 FIFA World Cup and had the honour of captaining England in their 3-0 victory over the United States in November 2018 in the Wayne Rooney Foundation International. He passed the armband to Rooney when he came on as a 58th minute substitute in the game for Jesse Lingard.

DECLAN RICE

Position: Midfielder **Date of Birth:** January 14, 1999
Place of Birth: Kingston-upon-Thames **Current Club:** West Ham United
England Debut: March 22, 2019 v Czech Republic (H)

Declan Rice played in three senior friendlies for the Republic of Ireland before committing his international future to England in February 2019. A month later he was included in Gareth Southgate's squad for their matches against Czech Republic and Montenegro, coming on as a 63rd minute substitute to make his debut against the former and while he started against the latter. He travelled to the UEFA Nations League finals in Portugal, playing 105 minutes of the semi-final clash against the Netherlands which went to extra-time.

RUBEN LOFTUS-CHEEK

Position: Midfielder **Date of Birth:** January 23, 1996
Place of Birth: London **Current Club:** Chelsea
England Debut: November 10, 2017 v Germany (H)

Ruben was just 17 when he made his senior debut for Chelsea against Sporting CP in the UEFA Champions League in December 2014. The midfielder received his first international experience at U16 level, captaining England's triumphant Victory Shield side in 2011. He was named best player at the 2016 Toulon Tournament and scored the winner for the U21s in their 2-1 success over France in the final. Ruben was named as Man of the Match on his Three Lions debut in 2017 and was included in Gareth Southgate's 23-man squad for the FIFA World Cup the following year.

HARRY KANE

Position: Forward **Date of Birth:** July 28, 1993
Place of Birth: London **Current Club:** Tottenham Hotspur
England Debut: March 27, 2015 v Lithuania (H)

In November 2018, at the age of 25, England captain Harry Kane scored his 20th goal in just his 35th appearance for England, prompting suggestions he could one day equal or surpass Wayne Rooney's record-breaking tally of 53 strikes for the Three Lions. The Tottenham Hotspur forward netted after just 80 seconds of his senior international debut against Lithuania in March 2015 having been introduced as a substitute for Rooney. He won the Golden Boot award at the 2018 FIFA World Cup with six strikes in as many games, while his 85th minute winner against Croatia in November 2018 booked England's place at the 2019 UEFA Nations League finals.

MARCUS RASHFORD

Position: Forward **Date of Birth:** October 31, 1997
Place of Birth: Manchester **Current Club:** Manchester United
England Debut: May 27, 2016 v Australia (H)

Marcus Rashford made a goal-scoring debut for England, netting in the Three Lions' 2-1 victory over Australia at Sunderland A's Stadium of Light in May 2016. In doing so, he became the youngest player ever to score on his debut for England, aged just 18 years and 208 days old at the time. The Manchester United forward was also on target in the memorable 3-2 away win against Spain in October 2018 while his strike against the Netherlands at the 2019 UEFA Nations League finals took his tally to seven strikes in 32 international appearances.

JADON SANCHO

Position: Forward **Date of Birth:** March 25, 2000
Place of Birth: London **Current Club:** Borussia Dortmund
England Debut: October 12, 2018 v Croatia (A)

FIFA U17 World Cup winner Jadon Sancho has made quite an impression at Bundesliga club Borussia Dortmund, scoring 14 times in 55 matches in his first two seasons in professional football, having previously spent time with Watford and Manchester City as a youngster. He also made a real impact with England's various youth and development squads, netting seven times in 11 appearances for the U16s as well as scoring 14 goals in 18 games for the U17s and two in five matches for the U19s. His senior debut for the Three Lions came in a goalless draw in Croatia in October 2018 while he made two appearances at the 2019 UEFA Nations League finals, as he won his fifth and sixth caps respectively.

CALLUM WILSON

Position: Forward **Date of Birth:** February 27, 1992
Place of Birth: Coventry **Current Club:** AFC Bournemouth
England Debut: November 15, 2018 v United States (H)

Callum Wilson scored on his debut for England against the United States in November 2018, becoming the first AFC Bournemouth player to net for the Three Lions in the process. The former Coventry City frontman had previously made just one international appearance in an U21 international against France in November 2014. He won his second senior cap in England's 5-1 away win in Montenegro in March 2017 and his third against Switzerland at the 2019 UEFA Nations League finals.

RAHEEM STERLING

Position: Forward **Date of Birth:** December 8, 1994
Place of Birth: Kingston, Jamaica **Current Club:** Manchester City
England Debut: November 14, 2012 v Sweden (A)

Raheem Sterling has been a mainstay in the England squad since making his debut in a 4-2 defeat to Sweden in November 2012 when he was just 17 years of age. He has made over 50 appearances for the Three Lions to date and was included in the squad for the 2014 and 2018 FIFA World Cups, UEFA Euro 2016 and the UEFA Nations League finals in 2019. His first international goal came in a 4-0 victory over Lithuania in March 2015, while he bagged a memorable brace in a 3-2 away win in Spain in October 2018. The 2018-19 PFA Young Player of the Year scored his first hat-trick for England came in the 5-0 demolition of the Czech Republic in March 2019.

CALLUM HUDSON-ODOI

Position: Forward **Date of Birth:** November 7, 2000
Place of Birth: London **Current Club:** Chelsea
England Debut: March 22, 2019 v Czech Republic (H)

Callum became one of the youngest players to make an England debut, as he made his bow as a 70th-minute substitute in the 5-0 victory over the Czech Republic in March 2019, aged 18. In his second appearances for the Three Lions - and first start – he registered an assist in the 5-1 win in Montenegro. The forward had previously played for England at all levels between U16 and U19 and was a key member of the Young Lions' squad that won the FIFA U17 World Cup and made the final of the UEFA U17 Championship in 2017. Callum's breakthrough at club level came in January 2018, when he came on as a substitute in Chelsea's Emirates FA Cup match with Newcastle United to make his Blues debut.

ENGLAND QUIZ

Can you answer these 20 questions?

1) What year did England compete in the European Championship finals for the first time?

2) At which world-famous stadium did John Barnes score his wonder goal against Brazil in 1984?

3) Which nation did England face in their opening match at UEFA Euro 1988 and the 1990 FIFA World Cup?

4) Who scored England's extra time winner against Belgium at the 1990 FIFA World Cup?

5) Who scored England's second goal in their 2-0 win over Scotland at UEFA Euro 1996?

6) Which nation did England beat in a penalty shootout at UEFA Euro 1996?

7) Which England player was the top scorer at UEFA Euro 1996 with five goals in as many games?

8) Which stadium hosted the UEFA Euro 1996 Final between Germany and the Czech Republic?

9) Which city hosted the 2002 FIFA World Cup qualifier between Germany and England in September 2001?

10) In addition to David Beckham, which former Manchester United striker scored in England's 2-2 draw with Greece at Old Trafford in October 2001?

11) Which French club do Lionesses Lucy Bronze, Isobel Christiansen, Alex Greenwood and Nikita Parris play for?

12) What tournament did the Lionesses win in the United States in 2019?

13) Who scored England's opening goal at the 2019 FIFA Women's World Cup?

14) Who did England beat 3-0 in the quarter-final of the 2019 FIFA Women's World Cup?

15) Where was Lionesses' striker Toni Duggan born?

16) Who scored the opening goal in England's UEFA Nations League semi-final with the Netherlands in June 2019?

17) Which defender made his England debut on his home club ground, the King Power Stadium, in September 2018?

18) How many England matches did it take Harry Kane to score 20 goals for the Three Lions?

19) Which club do Ruben Loftus-Cheek and Callum Hudson-Odoi play for?

20) How many different cities will stage matches at UEFA Euro 2020?

ANSWERS ON PAGE 61

PHIL NEVILLE

As a player, Phil Neville was part of Manchester United's famous 'Class of '92', that won the FA Youth Cup in 1992. Phil, along with brother Gary and the likes of David Beckham, Nicky Butt, Ryan Giggs and Paul Scholes established themselves as first-team regulars at Old Trafford. They were all part of the squad that won the 'Treble' – the Premier League, the FA Cup and the UEFA Champions League – in 1998-99.

Neville made his first-team debut for Manchester United in a 5-2 FA Cup fourth round victory over Wrexham in January 1995. The defender went on to feature in a total of 386 matches for the club over a ten-year period, scoring eight times. During his time at Old Trafford he won six Premier League titles, three FA Cups, three FA Charity Shields, the Intercontinental Cup and the Champions League.

In August 2005 Neville signed for Everton, making his debut for the Toffees in a Champions League qualifier against Spanish side Villarreal. He became skipper of the Merseyside club in January 2007, following the departure of David Weir and captained them in their 2-1 defeat to Chelsea in the 2009 FA Cup Final. In 2013, having scored 5 goals in 303 appearances for Everton, the defender announced his retirement from playing.

Neville won 59 senior caps for England during his career, making his debut against China in May 1996. He was included in the Three Lions' squad for the European Championships in 1996, 2000 and 2004 but never featured in a World Cup squad. His last appearance for his country came in a 3-0 victory over Estonia at Wembley Stadium in October 2007.

MANAGER PROFILE

FULL NAME:
PHILIP JOHN NEVILLE

DATE OF BIRTH:
JANUARY 21, 1977

PLACE OF BIRTH:
BURY

ENGLAND WOMEN'S HEAD COACH:
SINCE JANUARY 2018

In February 2012 Neville assisted the England Under-21 coaching staff for a match against Belgium when then-manager Stuart Pearce temporarily took charge of the senior side. He was also part of the team's coaching staff at the 2013 UEFA U21 Championships.

Shortly after retiring from playing, Neville became first-team coach at Manchester United under newly appointed manager David Moyes. He left Old Trafford at the end of the 2013-14 campaign. Ahead of the following season Neville, along with his brother Gary and former Red Devils Giggs, Scholes and Butt, agreed a deal to buy then non-league side Salford City with the aim of establishing them as a Football League team – an ambition recognised in 2019. Along with Scholes, he briefly took caretaker charge of the team in January 2015 following the departure of manager Phil Power.

Neville joined Spanish side Valencia as a coach under manager Nuno Espírito Santo in July 2015. He briefly served under interim boss Voro before departing the club a year later. He was appointed as manager of the England women's senior team in January 2018 and his first match in charge of the Lionesses saw them storm to an impressive 4-1 victory over France at the SheBelieves Cup.

In August 2018 England confirmed their place at the 2019 FIFA Women's World Cup with a 3-0 victory in Wales that saw them top their qualifying group. The Lionesses enjoyed the perfect preparation for the tournament, winning the SheBelieves Cup in March 2019. The team performed brilliantly at the World Cup too, reaching the semi-finals of the competition before going down to a 2-1 defeat to the United States in Lyon.

WOMEN'S SENIOR TEAM PROFILES

KAREN BARDSLEY	LEAH WILLIAMSON	BETH MEAD
CARLY TELFORD	ABBIE MCMANUS	ISOBEL CHRISTIANSEN
MARY EARPS	RACHEL DALY	FRAN KIRBY
ELLIE ROEBUCK	KEIRA WALSH	TONI DUGGAN
LUCY BRONZE	JILL SCOTT	NIKITA PARRIS
ALEX GREENWOOD	JADE MOORE	JODIE TAYLOR
STEPH HOUGHTON	JORDAN NOBBS	ELLEN WHITE
MILLIE BRIGHT	GEORGIA STANWAY	
DEMI STOKES	LUCY STANIFORTH	

KAREN BARDSLEY

Position: Goalkeeper **Date of Birth:** October 14, 1984
Place of Birth: Santa Monica, United States **Current Club:** Manchester City
England Debut: March 9, 2005 v Northern Ireland (N)

Karen Bardsley was born in Santa Monica, California to English parents in October 1984. She played football for the Cal State Fullerton Titans during her time at California State University and plied her trade for the likes of Pali Blues, Sky Blue FC and Linkopings before joining Lincoln Ladies in the FA WSL in 2013. She signed for her current club Manchester City WFC a year later and has since made over 50 league appearances for them. Since making her England debut in a 4-0 victory over Northern Ireland at the Algarve Cup in 2005, Bardsley has played over 80 matches for the Lionesses and has been included in the squads for three FIFA Women's World Cups and three UEFA Women's European Championships.

CARLY TELFORD

Position: Goalkeeper **Date of Birth:** July 7, 1987
Place of Birth: Jesmond **Current Club:** Chelsea
England Debut: March 11, 2007 v Scotland (H)

Having previously represented England at U17, U19, U21 and U23 level, Carly Telford made her senior Lionesses debut in a 1-0 victory over Scotland at Wycombe Wanderers FC's Adams Park ground in March 2007. Telford was included in squads for the 2007 and 2015 FIFA Women's World Cups and well as UEFA Women's Euro 2017, but didn't feature during those tournaments. She started in three matches at the 2019 FIFA World Cup, keeping a clean sheet on her competition bow against Argentina in a 1-0 win.

MARY EARPS

Position: Goalkeeper **Date of Birth:** March 7, 1993
Place of Birth: Nottingham **Current Club:** Manchester United
England Debut: June 11, 2017 v Switzerland (A)

While Mary Earps received her first England call-up for a match against Montenegro in April 2014, it wasn't until June 2017 that the goalkeeper finally got to make her Lionesses debut in a 4-0 win in Switzerland. Earps' club career has seen her represent the likes of Leicester City, Doncaster Rovers Belles, Bristol Academy, Reading and German giants VfL Wolgsburg, while she signed for Manchester United in the summer of 2019. Four of her five caps at the time of writing have come since the appointment of Phil Neville as England Head Coach, who included her in the squads for the SheBelieves Cup and the FIFA Women's World Cup in 2019.

ELLIE ROEBUCK

Position: Goalkeeper **Date of Birth:** September 23, 1999
Place of Birth: Sheffield **Current Club:** Manchester City
England Debut: November 8, 2018 v Austria (A)

Ellie Roebuck was a member of Sheffield United Girls' Centre of Excellence before joining Manchester City in 2016, for whom she signed her first professional contract in January 2018. The 5ft 8½ in goalkeeper was part of the Young Lionesses squad that finished third at the 2018 FIFA U20 Women's World Cup before making her senior England debut as a substitute for Mary Earps in a 3-0 win in Austria in November 2018. Her first start for the Lionesses came in a 2-1 win over Spain in April 2019.

LUCY BRONZE

Position: Defender **Date of Birth:** October 28, 1991
Place of Birth: Berwick-upon-Tweed
Current Club: Lyon
England Debut: June 26, 2013 v Japan (H)

Lucy Bronze is widely acknowledged as one of the finest right-backs in the women's game right now and was named as the PFA Women's Player of the Year in 2014 and 2017. She moved to French side Olympique Lyon in August 2017, where she has won two Division 1 Féminine and two UEFA Women's Champions League titles to date. With over 75 caps for England, the defender was included in the Lionesses squad for the 2013 and 2017 UEFA Women's European Championships as well as the 2015 FIFA Women's World Cup. At the 2019 FIFA Women's World Cup, she won the Silver Ball as the tournament's second-best player, after the United States' Megan Rapinoe.

ALEX GREENWOOD

Position: Defender **Date of Birth:** September 7, 1993
Place of Birth: Liverpool **Current Club:** Lyon
England Debut: March 5, 2014 v Italy (N)

With over 40 caps to her name, Alex Greenwood represented England at the 2015 FIFA Women's World Cup and the UEFA Women's Euro 2017. She also featured in four of England's seven matches at the 2019 FIFA Women's Cup, netting once with a controlled, left-footed effort against Cameroon in the round of 16. The former Manchester United Women's captain had previously scored for the Lionesses in a 10-0 win over Montenegro in September 2014 and against Serbia in a 7-0 triumph in June 2016.

STEPH HOUGHTON

Position: Defender **Date of Birth:** April 23, 1988
Place of Birth: Durham **Current Club:** Manchester City
England Debut: March 8, 2007 v Russia (H)

Lionesses skipper Steph Houghton has over 100 caps to her name having first represented England in a 6-0 win over Russia in Milton Keynes in March 2007. She missed the 2007 FIFA Women's World Cup and UEFA Women's Euro 2009 through injury but has featured at every major tournament since. She captained England to third and fourth place finishes at the 2015 and 2019 FIFA World Cups respectively, as well as skippering the side which reached the semi-finals of UEFA Euro 2017. While defending is her first priority, she has scored a number of important goals for England over the years including strikes against Norway and Cameroon at the 2015 and 2019 FIFA World Cups respectively. She was appointed a Member of the Order of the British Empire (MBE) in the 2016 New Year Honours for services to football.

MILLIE BRIGHT

Position: Defender **Date of Birth:** August 21, 1993
Place of Birth: Killamarsh **Current Club:** Chelsea
England Debut: September 20, 2016 v Belgium (A)

After the disappointment of missing out on the 2019 SheBelieves Cup triumph through injury, Millie Bright was Steph Houghton's regular central-defensive partner at that year's FIFA Women's World Cup, featuring in five of the seven matches at the tournament. Previously, the Chelsea defender - who made her Lionesses debut in a 2-0 win in Belgium in September 2016 – was selected in all five of the Lionesses' matches at UEFA Women's Euro 2017. At club level, the former England U19 and U23 international is a two-time FA WSL and SSE Women's FA Cup winner.

DEMI STOKES

Position: Defender **Date of Birth:** December 12, 1991
Place of Birth: Dudley Current Club: Manchester City
England Debut: January 17, 2014 v Norway (N)

Demi Stokes was part of the ultra-talented Young Lionesses side that won the 2009 UEFA Women's Under-19 Championships in Belarus, starting in the 2-0 victory over Sweden in the final alongside the likes of Lucy Bronze, Jordan Nobbs and Toni Duggan. She made her senior debut in a friendly match with Norway in La Manga, Spain in January 2014 and since then, has become the Lionesses regular pick at left-back. Her first international goal came in a 9-0 victory over Montenegro in a 2015 FIFA Women's World Cup

LEAH WILLIAMSON

Position: Defender **Date of Birth:** March 29, 1997
Place of Birth: Milton Keynes **Current Club:** Arsenal
England Debut: June 8, 2018 v Russia (A)

Leah Williamson joined Arsenal's Centre of Excellence as a nine-year-old and still remains with the north London club, for whom she made her debut against Birmingham City in the UEFA Women's Champions League in 2014. Having featured for England at youth and development stages between U15 and U23, the defender first appeared for the senior side as a substitute in a 3-1 victory in Russia in June 2018. She made her FIFA Women's World Cup debut from the bench, coming on in the round of 16 match against Cameroon to win her eighth senior cap.

ABBIE McMANUS

Position: Defender **Date of Birth:** January 14, 1993
Place of Birth: Prestwich **Current Club:** Manchester United
England Debut: March 1, 2018 v France (N)

Shortly before travelling with England to the 2019 FIFA Women's World Cup in France, Abbie McManus announced that she was leaving Manchester City for rivals Manchester United – the club she had supported as a child. The defender featured in three matches at France 2019, starting in the second group stage fixture against Argentina. She also started two of England's matches at the 2019 SheBelieves Cup, which saw the Lionesses win the tournament.

RACHEL DALY

Position: Defender/Forward **Date of Birth:** December 6, 1991
Place of Birth: Harrogate **Current Club:** Houston Dash
England Debut: June 4, 2016 v Serbia (H)

Capable of playing in defence or attack, Rachel Daly scored on her England debut in a 7-0 victory over Serbia in a UEFA Women's Euro 2017 qualifier in June 2016. She has since been included in Lionesses squads for the 2018 and 2019 SheBelieves Cup and the 2019 FIFA Women's World Cup. The former Leeds United and Lincoln Ladies player moved to the United States in 2013 and has previously represented club sides Los Angeles Strikers, LA Blues and SoCal FC. She was voted current club Houston Dash's most valuable player in 2018 after scoring ten goals in 24 matches.

KEIRA WALSH

Position: Midfielder **Date of Birth:** April 8, 1997
Place of Birth: Rochdale **Current Club:** Manchester City
England Debut: November 28, 2017 v Kazakhstan (H)

Less than 12 months on from making her England debut, Keira Walsh captained the Lionesses for the first time in a 6-0 win over Kazakhstan in September 2018, aged just 21 at the time. The midfielder started in all three of England's matches at the 2019 SheBelieves Cup and gained widespread plaudits for her defence-splitting assist for Beth Mead's goal in 3-0 win over Japan at the tournament. She featured in five matches at the FIFA Women's World Cup later a few months later. At club level, Walsh was part of the Manchester City side that won the FA WSL title in 2016, the SSE Women's FA Cup in 2017 and the Continental League Cup in 2019.

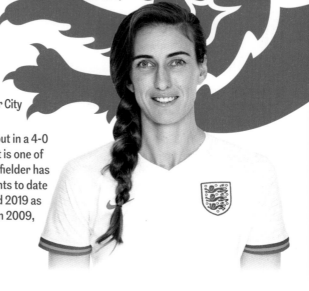

JILL SCOTT

Position: Midfielder **Date of Birth:** February 2, 1987
Place of Birth: Sunderland **Current Club:** Manchester City
England Debut: August 31, 2006 v Netherlands (H)

Having played over 140 matches since making her debut in a 4-0 victory over the Netherlands in August 2006, Jill Scott is one of just 11 Lionesses centurions. The Manchester City midfielder has been selected in the squad for seven major tournaments to date – the FIFA Women's World Cup in 2007, 2011, 2015 and 2019 as well as the UEFA Women's European Championships in 2009, 2013 and 2017.

JADE MOORE

Position: Midfielder **Date of Birth:** October 22, 1990
Place of Birth: Worksop **Current Club:** Reading
England Debut: February 28, 2012 v Finland (N)

Jade Moore was a member of England's squad that won the UEFA Women's Under-19 Championship in 2009. After making her Lionesses' debut against Finland, she scored on her second international appearance against Italy at the 2012 Cyprus Cup . Moore featured in Lionesses squads at the 2013 and 2017 UEFA Women's European Championships and the 2015 and 2019 FIFA Women's World Cups. She played in four matches at the latter tournament, with her start against Sweden in the third-place play-off marking her 50th international appearance.

JORDAN NOBBS

Position: Midfielder **Date of Birth:** December 8, 1992
Place of Birth: Stockton-on-Tees **Current Club:** Arsenal
England Debut: March 6, 2013 v Italy (N)

Jordan Nobbs was denied the opportunity of featuring at the 2019 FIFA Women's World Cup after rupturing her anterior cruciate ligament in February 2019. The midfielder instead worked as a pundit at the tournament for BBC Sport. Nobbs made her Lionesses debut in a 3-0 victory over Croatia at Walsall's Bescot Stadium in September 2012 and scored in her second international appearance – a 4-2 victory over Italy at the Cyprus Cup in March 2013. Since then, she has played over 50 times for her country and was voted England Player of the Year for 2016 at The FA Women's Football Awards.

GEORGIA STANWAY

Position: Midfielder **Date of Birth:** January 3, 1999
Place of Birth: Barrow-in-Furness **Current Club:** Manchester City
England Debut: November 8, 2018 v Austria (A)

Georgia Stanway was the joint top-goal scorer at the 2018 FIFA Under-20 World Cup in France with six strikes, as the Young Lionesses finished third at the tournament. Later that year, she scored on her senior England debut in a 3-0 win over Austria. At the end of the 2018-19 season, the Manchester City midfielder was named as the PFA Women's Young Player of the Year. She was the youngest outfield player to be included in Phil Neville's squad for the 2019 FIFA Women's World Cup and went on to feature in five matches.

LUCY STANIFORTH

Position: Midfielder **Date of Birth:** October 2, 1992
Place of Birth: York **Current Club:** Birmingham City
England Debut: September 4, 2018 v Kazakhstan (A)

In the same year she departed Sunderland for current club Birmingham City, Lucy Staniforth scored on her Lionesses debut in a 3-0 win against Kazakhstan in September 2018. She netted in the Lionesses' 3-0 triumph over Japan at the 2019 SheBelieves Cup and featured as a substitute in the 3-0 success against Cameroon at the 2019 FIFA World Cup.

BETH MEAD

Position: Forward **Date of Birth:** May 9, 1995
Place of Birth: Whitby **Current Club:** Arsenal
England Debut: April 6, 2018 v Wales (H)

Beth Mead was England's top assist maker at the 2019 FIFA Women's World Cup, as she laid on three goals for her teammates at the tournament. The forward is a relatively recent addition to the Lionesses squad, making her debut against Wales in April 2018. Her efforts against Brazil and Japan helped England to their 2019 SheBelieves Cup success while her strike in 2-1 victory against Spain in April 2019 was her fifth goal for her country. Mead was the winner of the PFA Women's Young Player of the Year in 2016.

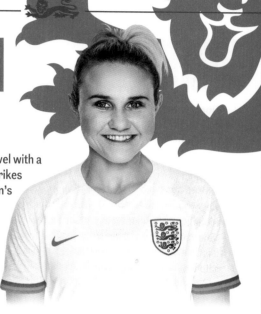

ISOBEL CHRISTIANSEN

Position: Midfielder/Forward **Date of Birth:** September 20, 1991
Place of Birth: Macclesfield **Current Club:** Lyon
England Debut: September 21, 2015 v Estonia (A)

Isobel Christiansen announced herself at senior international level with a goal on her debut in an 8-0 win in Estonia in September 2015. Strikes in home and away victories over Kazakhstan in 2019 FIFA Women's World Cup qualifying matches helped the Lionesses reach the finals but an injury sustained in England's 3-0 win over Japan at the 2019 SheBelieves Cup saw the 2016 PFA Women's Players' Player of the Year ruled her out of France 2019.

FRAN KIRBY

Position: Forward **Date of Birth:** June 29, 1993
Place of Birth: Reading **Current Club:** Chelsea
England Debut: August 3, 2014 v Sweden 2014 (H)

In addition to her strike against Sweden in the third-place play-off, Fran Kirby completed most key passes for England at the 2019 FIFA Women's World Cup, with eleven in total. Her debut for the Lionesses came against Sweden, as she got the second goal in a 4-0 win in August 2014. She announced herself on the global stage with a memorable solo effort against Mexico at the 2015 FIFA World Cup while she netted in a 2-0 triumph over Spain at UEFA Women's Euro 2017. Kirby was voted both PFA and FWA Women's Players' Player of the Year in 2017-18.

TONI DUGGAN

Position: Forward **Date of Birth:** July 25, 1991
Place of Birth: Liverpool **Current Club:** Atletico Madrid
England Debut: September 19, 2012 v Croatia (H)

Shortly after the 2019 FIFA Women's World Cup, which saw Toni Duggan feature in three matches at the tournament, the Liverpool-born forward announced her departure from Barcelona ahead of a move to Atletico Madrid. In two seasons with the Catalan giants, Duggan netted 29 times in 72 appearance and won both the Copa de la Reina and Copa Catalunya. The striker made her England debut in a 3-0 win over Croatia in 2012 and has scored many important goals for her country, including hat-tricks against Turkey in September 2013 and Montenegro in April 2014. She has been a key member of Phil Neville's squad since his appointment as manager in January 2018 and was handed the Lionesses armband for the first time in the 3-0 win over Austria later that year.

NIKITA PARRIS

Position: Forward **Date of Birth:** March 10, 1994
Place of Birth: Toxteth **Current Club:** Lyon
England Debut: June 4, 2016 v Serbia (H)

After featuring in all seven of the Lionesses' matches at the 2019 FIFA Women's World Cup, Nikita Parris completed a transfer from Manchester City to Lyon. The forward departed the Citizens having won two SSE Women's FA Cups, two Continental Cups and the FA WSL title during her time at the club. Parris has been a regular feature of the England team since she came on as a substitute to make her debut in a 7-0 victory over Serbia in June 2016. She has scored many important goals in that time, including the winner against Portugal at UEFA Women's Euro 2017 and a strike against the United States in the successful 2019 SheBelieves Cup

JODIE TAYLOR

Position: Forward **Date of Birth:** May 17, 1986
Place of Birth: Birkenhead **Current Club:** Reign
England Debut: August 3, 2014 v Sweden (H)

Jodie Taylor has been a regular source of goals for England since making her Lionesses debut in a 4-0 victory over Sweden in August 2014. Her first strikes came in a 3-0 victory over Australia at the 2015 Cyprus Cup, in which she scored a hat-trick. She was also on target in a 2-1 win against Canada at the 2015 FIFA Women's World Cup, while she netted five times at UEFA Women's Euro 2017 - including a hat-trick in a 6-0 triumph over Scotland in Utrecht – to land the tournament's Golden Boot. She scored her 18th international goal to give the Lionesses a 1-0 success over Argentina at the 2019 FIFA Women's World Cup and made three appearances at the finals.

ELLEN WHITE

Position: Forward **Date of Birth:** May 9, 1989
Place of Birth: Aylesbury **Current Club:** Manchester City
England Debut: March 25, 2010 v Austria (H)

With six goals in six matches, Ellen White was the joint-top goal-scorer at the 2019 FIFA Women's World Cup - along with the United States' Megan Rapinoe and Alex Morgan - which saw her collect the Bronze Boot. White has been a prolific goal scorer throughout her England career, netting on her senior debut against Austria in March 2010. She marked her first appearance at FIFA Women's World Cup by scoring an audacious lob against eventual tournament winners Japan in 2011. She was named England Women's Player of the Year in 2011, following up that success again in 2018. Her strike in the 2-1 defeat to the United States at the 2019 FIFA World Cup was White's 34th goal for her country.

WORDSEARCH

Find the surnames of these England European Championship goalscorers.

```
C Q S E L O H C S D R D M L M E
D R A R R E G P X W P J Q Y G P
K D R R Q Q R B C W A V N D X N
T R R E H V J N E H B L I K M Y
P A O F R B D L V G A R C W F V
M P B N J A B T N C R R G O X V
A M S J M E E I S U P A L N T W
H A O M C M K H T R S L D T J T
G L N K B O T S S C U R A Q O G
N S C C O G T Q O G D H R T M N
I M N R M T R I J G P J M L T D
R A B Z O O G C A R R O L L D K
E D P C O N X L K J N F B V I H
H A S N E D K C O C D O O W E B
S E E T K Z R S N I K L I W R R
L Y Q W H X O W E N X V A R D Y
```

ADAMS	ROBSON
BROOKING	ROONEY
CARROLL	SCHOLES
CHARLTON	SHEARER
DIER	SHERINGHAM
GASCOIGNE	STURRIDGE
GERRARD	VARDY
HURST	WALCOTT
LAMPARD	WELBECK
LESCOTT	WILKINS
OWEN	WOODCOCK
PLATT	

WHAT'S THE SCORE?

Can you fill in the scoreboards from these famous England matches?

A) FIFA WORLD CUP 1966
30 JULY 1966 –
WEMBLEY STADIUM

[ ] [ ]

ENGLAND   WEST GERMANY

B) UEFA EURO 1996
18 JUNE 1996 –
WEMBLEY STADIUM

[ ] [ ]

ENGLAND   NETHERLANDS

C) FIFA WORLD CUP 2002 QUALIFYING
1 SEPTEMBER 2001 –
OLYMPIASTADION

[ ] [ ]

GERMANY   ENGLAND

D) FIFA WORLD CUP 2018
24 JUNE 2018 –
NIZHNY NOVGOROD STADIUM

[ ] [ ]

ENGLAND   PANAMA

E) UEFA NATIONS LEAGUE 2018/19
15 OCTOBER 2018 –
ESTADIO BENITO VILLAMARIN

[ ] [ ]

SPAIN   ENGLAND

F) FIFA WOMEN'S WORLD CUP 2019
22 JUNE 2019 –
STADE DE NICE

[ ] [ ]

ENGLAND   CAMEROON

FOR ANSWERS SEE PAGE 61.

SEND HER VICTORIOUS!

A series of excellent performances saw Phil Neville's Lionesses crowned 2019 SheBelieves Cup Champions.

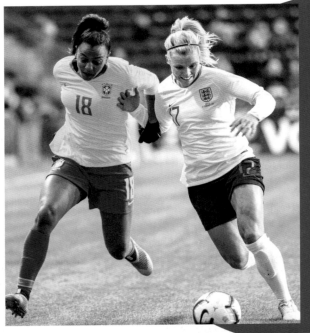

England 2-1 Brazil

February 27, 2019
Talen Energy Stadium, Chester, Pennsylvania

A stunning, long-range strike from Beth Mead saw England claim victory in their opening match at the 2019 SheBelieves Cup. The Lionesses had gone behind early on, when Lucy Bronze was adjudged to have fouled Marta in the penalty area and Andressa slotted home the resulting spot-kick. Phil Neville's team levelled three minutes into the second half though, when Ellen White slotted home after a fine through-ball from Fran Kirby prior to Mead's winner from the edge of the Brazilian penalty area 15 minutes from time.

United States 2-2 England

March 2, 2019
Nissan Stadium, Nashville, Tennessee

England faced tournament hosts United States in their second match at the SheBelieves Cup, who were ranked number one in the world at that time. Megan Rapinoe gave the Stars and Stripes the lead just after the half hour mark with a firmly struck half-volley. Steph Houghton levelled for the Lionesses moments later, curling an indirect free-kick from just inside the States' penalty area into back of the net. Seven minutes after the break, Nikita Parris got on the end of a Fran Kirby through ball before coolly finishing past goalkeeper Adrianna Franch. Tobin Heath equalised for the hosts with 23 minutes of the 90 remaining as an entertaining encounter ended all square.

Japan 0-3 England

March 5, 2019
Raymond James Stadium, Tampa, Florida

The SheBelieves Cup top two went head-to-head in the penultimate match of the tournament, with the winners of the game knowing they would collect the trophy. England got off to the perfect start, with Jodie Taylor playing the ball into the path of Lucy Staniforth to finish from outside of the Japan penalty area after just 13 minutes. Karen Carney doubled the Lionesses' lead 11 minutes later with a header while Mead got her second goal of the tournament to make it three without reply before half time. A professional second-half display saw England keep a clean sheet and confirm their SheBelieves Cup 2019 triumph. The United States beat Brazil 1-0 in the final match of the competition.

FINAL STANDINGS

Pos		Pla	W	D	L	GF	GA	GD	Pts
1	ENGLAND	3	2	1	0	7	3	+4	7
2	UNITED STATES	3	1	2	0	5	4	+1	5
3	JAPAN	3	1	1	1	5	6	-1	4
4	BRAZIL	3	0	0	3	2	6	-4	0

2019 FIFA WOMEN'S WORLD CUP

A memorable year for Phil Neville's Lionesses continued as England got to the semi-finals of the 2019 FIFA Women's World Cup

England 2-1 Scotland
FIFA Women's World Cup Group D
June 9, 2019
Allianz Riviera, Nice

A Nikita Parris penalty saw England take a 14th-minute lead in their opening FIFA Women's World Cup Group D fixture against Scotland in Nice. The spot-kick was awarded with the assistance of the Video Assistant Referee (VAR), after Fran Kirby's cross hit Nicola Docherty's arm. The Lionesses doubled their lead before the break when Ellen White seized on a loose ball in the Scottish penalty area and finished first-time with her left foot.

With eleven minutes of the match remaining, Claire Emslie halved Scotland's deficit, beating Karen Bardsley from close range. But Phil Neville's team held on for a 2-1 win and three important points.

England Line-Up: Bardsley, Bronze, Houghton (c), Bright (McManus), Greenwood, Walsh, Kirby (Stanway), Scott, Parris, White, Mead (Carney), White

England 1-0 Argentina
FIFA Women's World Cup Group D
June 14, 2019
Stade Océane, Le Havre

England were awarded a first-half penalty in Le
Havre when Alex Greenwood was tripped by Ruth
Bravo inside the Argentinian 18-yard-box, but
goalkeeper Vanina Correa produced an excellent
save from Nikita Parris' resulting spot-kick during
a goalless first period.

Correa also kept out efforts from Beth Mead and
Jodie Taylor before the Lionesses finally broke the
deadlock just after the hour mark. A swift England
attack involving Jill Scott and Kirby allowed Mead
to cross from the left and Taylor was able to slot
home from close range after making a perfectly-
timed run into the six-yard-box.

The 1-0 win confirmed England's progress to the
knockout phase of the tournament with one group
match remaining.

England Line-Up: Telford, Bronze, Houghton (c),
McManus, Greenwood, Mead (Stanway), Moore,
Scott, Kirby (Carney), Taylor, Parris (Daly), Taylor

Japan 0-2 England
FIFA Women's World Cup
Group D
June 19, 2019
Allianz Riviera, Nice

A brace from White saw England beat 2011 world champions Japan in Nice to top the Group D table. The striker's first goal arrived on 14 minutes as she slotted the ball past goalkeeper Ayaka Yamashita after a neat pass from Georgia Stanway. Prior to that, Bardsley made an incredible save from Kumi Yokoyama's 35-yard free-kick, tipping the goal-bound ball onto the crossbar.

White doubled the Lionesses' advantage with six minutes of normal time remaining with another left-footed finish from substitute Karen Carney's through ball.

England Line-Up: Bardsley, Bronze, Houghton (c), Bright, Stokes, Scott, Walsh (Moore), Stanway (Carney), Daly, White, Duggan (Parris), White

GROUP D – FINAL STANDINGS

Pos		Pld	W	D	L	GF	GA	GD	Pts
1	ENGLAND	3	3	0	0	5	1	+4	9
2	JAPAN	3	1	1	1	2	3	-1	4
3	ARGENTINA	3	0	2	1	3	4	-1	2
4	BRAZIL	3	0	1	2	5	7	-2	1

England 3-0 Cameroon
FIFA Women's World Cup
Round of 16
June 23, 2019
Stade du Hainaut, Valenciennes

England took a 14th-minute lead in their round of 16 clash with Cameroon. An indirect free-kick was awarded to the Lionesses just outside the African nation's six-yard-box following a back pass. Toni Duggan tapped the resulting set-piece into the path of skipper Steph Houghton, who placed a precise shot into the bottom corner of Annette Ngo Ndom's goal.

White's red-hot goalscoring form at the Women's World Cup continued with calm finish after a pass from Bronze. Her effort was originally flagged for offside, but referee Qin

Liang awarded the goal after a VAR review. A 3-0 victory was confirmed on 58 minutes when Greenwood finished a well-worked set piece, hitting a low corner from Duggan into the back of the net with a first-time shot.

England Line-Up: Bardsley, Bronze, Houghton (c), Bright, Greenwood, Walsh, Kirby, Scott (Staniforth), Parris (Williamson), Duggan, White (Taylor)

England 3-0 Norway
FIFA Women's World Cup Quarter-Final
June 27, 2019
Stade Océane, Le Havre

A third-minute goal from Scott set the tone as England cruised to a 3-0 victory over Norway in their Le Havre quarter-final. The Manchester City midfielder swept home after a fine cross from Bronze. White hit the post moments later before doubling the Lionesses lead five minutes from the break with a close-range finish after a pass from Parris.

Bronze made it three 12 minutes into the second half with a rocket from outside of the penalty area after substitute Mead laid a free-kick into her path. The goal was met with applause from former men's senior team captain David Beckham, who was watching in the stands. Parris had a late penalty saved by Norway goalkeeper Ingrid Hjelmseth after Maria Thorisdottir's foul on Houghton. It mattered not as England's World Cup adventure continued.

England Line-Up: Bardsley, Bronze, Houghton (c), Bright, Stokes, Walsh, Kirby (Stanway), Scott, Parris (Daly), White, Duggan (Mead), White

England 1-2 United States
FIFA Women's World Cup Semi-Final
July 2, 2019
Parc Olympique Lyonnais, Lyon

Reigning world champions the United States made a bright start to their semi-final against England in Lyon, with Rose Lavelle forcing Carly Telford to make an excellent save early on before Christen Press gave them the lead with a 10th-minute header.

The Lionesses were on level terms nine minutes later as White touched in from a Mead cross to become the first-ever England player to score in five consecutive World Cup matches. Alex Morgan restored the States' lead just after the half-hour mark.

Phil Neville's team put on a spirited performance in the second half and thought they'd levelled through White's second 'goal' of the match, only for her effort to be ruled out after a VAR review. England were awarded a penalty late on, when Becky Sauerbrunn tripped White in the United States' 18-yard-box. However, Houghton's 86th-minute spot-kick was saved by goalkeeper Alyssa Naeher to deny the Lionesses the opportunity of taking the match to extra time.

England Line-Up: Telford, Bronze, Houghton (c), Bright, Stokes, Walsh (Moore), Scott, Mead (Kirby), Daly (Stanway), Parris, White

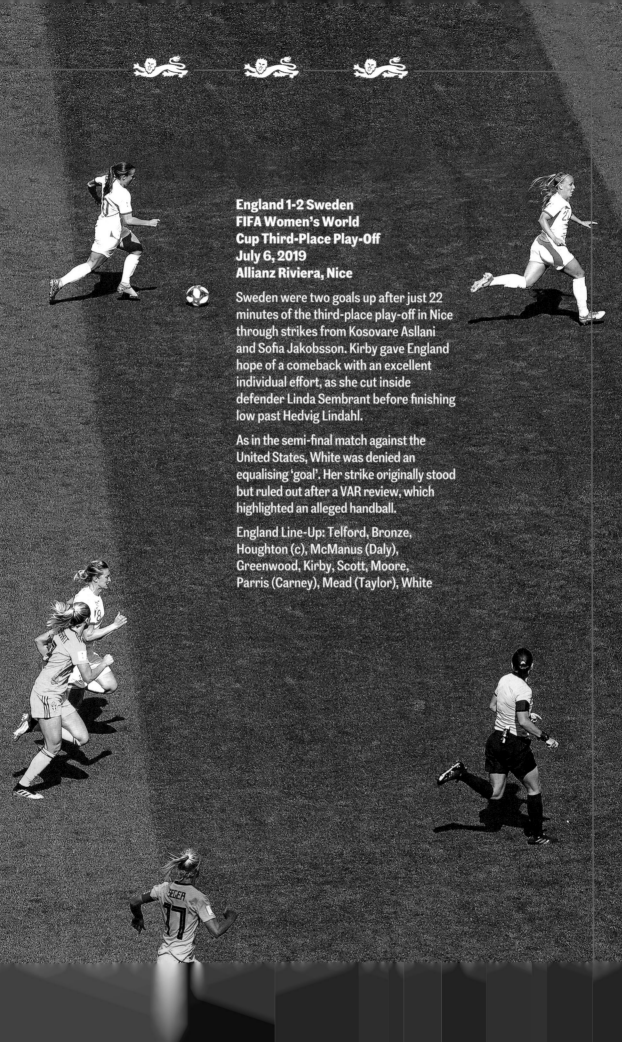

England 1-2 Sweden
FIFA Women's World
Cup Third-Place Play-Off
July 6, 2019
Allianz Riviera, Nice

Sweden were two goals up after just 22 minutes of the third-place play-off in Nice through strikes from Kosovare Asllani and Sofia Jakobsson. Kirby gave England hope of a comeback with an excellent individual effort, as she cut inside defender Linda Sembrant before finishing low past Hedvig Lindahl.

As in the semi-final match against the United States, White was denied an equalising 'goal'. Her strike originally stood but ruled out after a VAR review, which highlighted an alleged handball.

England Line-Up: Telford, Bronze, Houghton (c), McManus (Daly), Greenwood, Kirby, Scott, Moore, Parris (Carney), Mead (Taylor), White

AWARD WINNERS

In January 2019, Harry Kane was announced as the winner of the 2018 England Men's Player of the Year. The Tottenham Hotspur striker enjoyed a fantastic 12 months representing the Three Lions, scoring eight goals in 12 appearances during the year. Six of those goals came at the 2018 FIFA World Cup, as Kane helped England reach the semi-final of the competition for the first time in 28 years. He also became the first Englishman to claim the tournament's Golden Boot since Gary Lineker in 1986.

Another major international highlight for Kane in 2018 was his 85th minute winner in England's 2-1 triumph over Croatia that saw the Three Lions book their place in the finals of the UEFA Nations League.

Dominic Calvert-Lewin was selected as the 2018 England Men's Under-21s Player of the Year by The FA's broadcast partner BT Sport. The Everton forward scored five goals in seven appearances for England Under-21's during the calendar year. He previously netted six times in 14 matches for the Three Lions' Under-20 side between 2016 and 2017, with whom he won the FIFA U20 World Cup in 2017.

Beth Mead scooped the 2018 England Young Women's Player of the Year award, having made her senior international debut against Wales in April of that year. Her first goals for the national team came as she got a brace on her first start for the Lionesses in a 6-0 win in Kazakhstan that September.

The 2018 England Women's Player of the Year award went to Ellen White, who scored two goals in three appearances at the SheBelieves Cup during the year. White previously took the accolade back in 2011.

GET INVOLVED! THE FA SUPER KICKS

Introducing Kicker and some cool FA SuperKicks challenges!

Hi, I'm Kicker, your FA SuperKicks coach, guide and mentor! Here are some fun outdoor challenges to help hone your football skills and improve your balance and movement. See how you get on and whether you can better your score each time you retry a challenge.

Good luck!
Kicker

PLAY FOOTBALL

FIRST TIME FINISHING (SCORING CHALLENGE)

10 MINS/OUTDOOR CHALLENGE/LEVEL ONE

You Will Need:
A safe space, a football and a goal (two jumpers will do)

Challenge:
With your back to the goal, gently roll the ball away and before the ball stops moving, turn and shoot with your first touch. How many goals can you score?!

Handy Tips:
Know where the goal is before you shoot and try to get your standing foot in line with the ball when you strike it. Kick through the ball for more power.

BATTLE RACE (DRIBBLING CHALLENGE)

5 MINS/OUTDOOR CHALLENGE/LEVEL ONE

You Will Need:
A friend, a safe outdoor space, two footballs and different targets.

Challenge:
Set out your targets on the ground and travel around the target area touching the ball with different parts of your foot. You score a point for each target you reach. However, no points are awarded if you and your friend arrive at the same target. Race around the area and try and get more points than your friend!

Handy Tips:
To help you get as many points as possible, keep your eyes out for where your friend is going as well as where you and your ball are travelling.

BULLSEYE (PASSING CHALLENGE)

10 MINS/OUTDOOR CHALLENGE/LEVEL ONE

You Will Need:
A football, a safe outdoor space and some markers to create a target area.

Challenge:
Mark out a target circle on the ground. Practice your accurate passing by trying to play the ball into the centre of the target. Take five attempts and score 50 points each time you land it inside the target. Try again and see if you can better your score!

Handy Tips:
If you are finding the challenge tricky, make the target area bigger. For a tougher challenge, make the target area smaller.

GET ACTIVE

BALANCE THE BALL (BALANCE CHALLENGE)

5 MINS/OUTDOOR CHALLENGE/LEVEL ONE

You Will Need:
A safe outdoor space and a football.

Challenge:
Try to balance the ball on a part of your body – it could be your hand, foot, elbow, even head! See how long you can hold the balance for. Try to hold the balance for longer each time you try the task.

Handy Tips:
If you are finding the challenge tricky, try balancing the ball on a different part of your body.

If you liked those challenges there are 100s more on The FA SuperKicks app. For more challenges, you can download today via the Apple App Store or Amazon App Store. More details and download links can be found at **www.thefa.com/SuperKicks**

WHEN FOOTBALL CAME HOME

As Wembley Stadium prepares to host seven UEFA Euro 2020 matches – including both semi-finals and the final on July 12, 2020 – we look back to 1996, when England had the honour of hosting the European Championships for the first time.

SWEET 16

UEFA Euro 1996 was the tenth edition of the European Championships and the first to feature 16 teams. Eight nations competed at the tournament between 1980 and 1992, while just four sides took part between 1960 and 1976. It was also the first championships where three points were awarded for a group stage win, compared to two points at previous tournaments.

Eight venues in eight cities across England staged Euro 1996 matches including the original Wembley Stadium and Villa Park, which hosted Group A fixtures featuring the Three Lions, Netherlands, Scotland and Switzerland. Group B contained Bulgaria, France, Romania and Spain – with their matches being played at Elland Road and St James' Park, while the Czech Republic, Germany, Italy and Russia went head-to-head in Group C with their games staged at Old Trafford and Anfield. Group D sides Croatia, Denmark, Portugal and Turkey completed the tournament line-up with Nottingham and Sheffield hosting their group matches, at the City Ground and Hillsborough respectively.

IT'S COMING HOME

The official anthem of UEFA Euro 1996 was 'We're In This Together' by Simply Red, who performed at both the opening and closing ceremonies of the tournament. The official song of the England team meanwhile was 'Three Lions (Football's Coming Home)' by (David) Baddiel & (Frank) Skinner & The Lightning Seeds.

Released as a cassette and CD single on May 20, 1996, 'Three Lions' was quickly embraced by England supporters, who sang it during the tournament and continue to belt out its lyrics at matches at home and abroad today. The song peaked at number one in UK Singles Chart during Euro 1996 and made a return to the top spot in 2018 as England reached the semi-finals of the FIFA World Cup that year.

BATTLE OF BRITAIN

Following a 1-1 draw with Switzerland in the opening match of the competition, England hosted Scotland at Wembley for the latest instalment of international football's oldest fixture. After a goalless first half, the game burst into life on 53 minutes as Alan Shearer headed in from a Gary Neville cross for his second goal of the tournament.

With less than 15 minutes of the match remaining, Scotland were awarded a penalty when Tony Adams felled Gordon Durie in the Three Lions' 18-yard-box, but goalkeeper David Seaman sprang to his right to make a remarkable save from Gary McAllister's resulting spot-kick. Moments later, Darren Anderton lofted the ball into the path of Paul Gascoigne to wrap up the game 2-0, with a phenomenal goal.

Born in Gateshead, Gascoigne represented England a total of 57 times between 1988 and 1998, scoring ten goals in the process. The midfielder - who played for club sides including Newcastle United, Tottenham Hotspur, Lazio, Rangers, Middlesbrough and Everton during his career – became a national treasure with his performances at the 1990 FIFA World Cup that helped inspire the Three Lions' run to the semi-finals. Six years later, sporting distinctive bleach-blonde hair, he was similarly impressive at Euro 1996.

THE SAS

Then-England manager Terry Venables' chosen strike partnership at the tournament was Spurs forward Teddy Sheringham and Blackburn Rovers' Alan Shearer. Dubbed the 'SAS' by sections of the British media during Euro 1996, due to their surname initials and shooting abilities, the pair scored seven goals between them at that summer's championships.

Their standout display came as England thrashed the Netherlands 4-1 to secure top-spot in Group A and progress to the quarter finals. The Three Lions took the lead after 23 minutes of the match at Wembley, when Shearer converted from the penalty spot after Paul Ince had been fouled by Danny Blind.

Six minutes into the second half, Sheringham made it two, heading in from a Gascoigne corner. The 'SAS' combined for the third goal of the evening as Sheringham feinted to shoot before sliding a pass into Shearer to fire past goalkeeper Edwin van der Sar for his brace. Sheringham completed a double of his own just after the hour mark, getting to the loose ball after Van der Sar was unable to hold a shot from Darren Anderton to score. Patrick Kluivert's late consolation for Holland ensured they qualified for the quarter finals along with England at the expense of Scotland.

Shearer finished as the top scorer at Euro 1996 with five goals in as many matches. Shortly after the tournament had finished, the former Southampton forward completed a move from Blackburn Rovers to Newcastle United for a then-world record transfer fee of £15m.

Sheringham netted eleven times in 51 appearances for England between 1993 and 2002. The London-born frontman was the subject of a major transfer himself in the summer of 1997 as he moved from Tottenham Hotspur to Manchester United. He went on to win three Premier League titles, the FA Cup, UEFA Champions League and the Intercontinental Cup during his time at Old Trafford.

A SAFE PAIR OF HANDS

If Shearer and Sheringham had been the stand-out performers in England's demolition of the Netherlands, it was goalkeeper David Seaman who was the hero of their quarter final encounter with Spain at Wembley Stadium.

With the match goalless after extra time, Seaman made a fantastic save from Miguel Angel Nadal in the resulting penalty shootout. Shearer, David Platt, Stuart Pearce and Gascoigne all scored for England while Fernando Hierro struck the woodwork as the Three Lions won 4-2 on spot-kicks. The Three Lions' triumph exorcised the ghosts of the 1990 FIFA World Cup for Pearce, who had his penalty save in the 4-3 semi-final penalty shootout defeat to West Germany, his fist-pumping celebration after his penalty went in against Spain perhaps reflecting both joy and relief!

Seaman, who spent much of his club career with Arsenal and also represented Peterborough

United, Birmingham City, Queens Park Rangers and Manchester City, made 75 appearances for England between 1988 and 2002. He featured at four major tournaments for the Three Lions, including the 1998 and 2002 FIFA World Cups and UEFA Euro 2000.

SO NEAR YET SO FAR

An epic semi-final between England and Germany at Wembley Stadium saw the hosts take the lead after just three minutes after Shearer headed in from a Gascoigne corner. Germany levelled at 13 minutes as Stefan Kuntz converted from a Thomas Helmer cross.

The match eventually went to extra time. The 'Golden Goal' system was in operation at the tournament, meaning whichever side scored first in the added period of 30 minutes of extra time would progress straight to the final. Anderton and Gascoigne both came agonisingly close to securing victory for England with Anderton striking Germany's goal frame while Gazza came within an inch of getting to a Shearer cross to put the ball into the back of an unguarded net.

With no further goals the match went to penalties, with Germany triumphing 6-5 on spot-kicks.

Germany went on to win a memorable tournament, beating the Czech Republic 2-1 in the final at Wembley. Oliver Bierhoff scored twice for the tournament winners, including the all-important Golden Goal in extra time.

ENGLAND'S GREATEST GOALS

There's no shortage of great goals in England's history. We pick out some of the most memorable throughout the years. Which favourite goals would you add to the list?

SIR GEOFF HURST

England 4-2 West Germany (after extra-time)
1966 FIFA World Cup Final
July 30, 1966 - Wembley Stadium, London

The 1966 FIFA World Cup Final was level at the end of the 90 minutes, with Geoff Hurst and Martin Peters having scored for the Three Lions while Helmut Haller and Wolfgang Weber were on target for Die Mannschaft.

In extra-time, Hurst was on target once again, before sealing his hat-trick and England's 4-2 victory with a memorable run and shot that is the first strike to be included on our list of 'Greatest Goals'. In the last minute of extra-time, the former West Ham United forward collected a long pass from club teammate Bobby Moore just inside the German half. He carried the ball into the penalty area before lashing a left-footed shot past goalkeeper Hans Tilkowski.

His goal gave rise to one of the most famous pieces of commentary of all-time as the BBC's Kenneth Wolstenholme described the action as follows: "And here comes Hurst. He's got... some people are on the pitch, they think it's all over. It is now! It's four!"

JOHN BARNES

Brazil 0-2 England
International Match
June 10, 1984 - Maracanã, Rio de Janeiro

John Barnes was just 20 years of age when he scored the first of his 11 England goals, during a career in which he made 79 international appearances between 1983 and 1995. And what a goal it was!

Just before half-time in a game against Brazil at the world-famous Maracanã stadium, Barnes collected a pass from Mark Hateley with his chest close to the left touchline. Sprinting past marker Leandro, the then-Watford player continued on a slalom run through the Brazilian defence before slotting the ball past goalkeeper Junior.

In a 2013 interview with talkSPORT, Barnes described watching replays of his effort in the Maracanã as "an out-of-body experience" because "I can't remember doing any of that"!

DAVID PLATT

**England 1-0 Belgium
(after extra-time)
1990 FIFA World Cup Round of 16
June 26, 1990
Stadio Renato Dall'Ara, Bologna**

After a goalless 90 minutes, England's round of 16 tie looked to be heading for a penalty shootout with the deadlock yet to be broken going into the closing seconds of extra time.

With just over a minute left to play, the Three Lions were awarded a free-kick in a promising position when Eric Gerets tripped Paul Gascoigne. 'Gazza' took the resulting free-kick, lofting it into the 18-yard-box. As the ball headed in his direction, substitute David Platt managed to escape the attention of his marker before swivelling and hitting an unstoppable volley past Michel Preud'homme.

"England have done it in the last minute of extra-time," declared BBC commentator John Motson as manager Sir Bobby Robson and his players celebrated one of the Three Lions' greatest World Cup moments.

PAUL GASCOIGNE

**England 2-0 Scotland
UEFA Euro 1996 Group Stage
June 15, 1996
Wembley Stadium, London**

Having first been played in 1872, England versus Scotland is the oldest international fixture in the world. The Three Lions went one up against their old rivals when the two sides met at Euro '96 thanks to an early header from Alan Shearer.

Eleven minutes from time, Paul Gascoigne – playing his club football for Scottish side Glasgow Rangers at the time – sealed victory for England with a truly memorable goal. Moments after David Seaman had saved a penalty from Gary McAllister, 'Gazza' collected a fine lofted pass from Darren Anderton. With his first touch, the midfielder flicked the ball over the head of defender Colin Hendry before rifling a right-footed volley past club mate Andy Gorman in the Scottish goal.

MICHAEL OWEN

England 2-2 Argentina
(after extra-time, Argentina win 4-3
on penalties)
FIFA World Cup Round of 16
June 30, 1998
Stade Geoffroy-Guichard,
Saint-Étienne

The round of 16 clash between England and Argentina was played at a frenetic pace from start to finish and saw a penalty awarded to both sides in the opening nine minutes. Gabriel Batistuta and Alan Shearer respectively converted from 12-yards.

The Three Lions took the lead after 16 minutes, with a remarkable goal from Michael Owen – who was just 18 at the time. Collecting a pass from David Beckham in the centre-circle, the then-Liverpool forward held off a challenge from Jose Chamot and turned Roberto Ayala before slamming the ball past Carlos Roa in the Argentina goal.

Javier Zanetti equalised for Argentina just before half-time on a night when Beckham was sent-off and Sol Campbell had a 'goal' disallowed. Despite a battling display – and Owen's wonder-strike - Glenn Hoddle's team were eventually beaten 4-3 in a penalty shootout.

STEVEN GERRARD

Germany 1-5 England
2002 FIFA World Cup Qualifier
September 1, 2001
Olympiastadion, Munich

England produced one of the most complete performances in their history to claim a 5-1 victory over Germany in 2001 – just their second triumph over Die Mannschaft since the 1966 FIFA World Cup Final. The night will be remembered for a Steven Gerrard wonder-goal, a Michael Owen hat-trick and a further strike from Emile Heskey – all of this after Carsten Jancker had given the home side a sixth-minute lead.

Gerrard put Sven-Göran Eriksson's side 2-1 up in the fourth minute of stoppage time at the end of the first half. David Beckham saw his initial free-kick from the edge of the German penalty area cleared before delivering a left-footed cross back into the box. Rio Ferdinand headed the ball into the path of the on-rushing Gerrard, who controlled it with his chest and struck it from all of 25 yards.

The former Liverpool midfielder later described the win as his best moment in an England shirt and his strike in the match as one of his top three goals for his country along with efforts against Macedonia in 2002 and Hungary in 2010.

DAVID BECKHAM

England 2-2 Greece
2002 FIFA World Cup Qualifier
October 6, 2001
Old Trafford, Manchester

With England requiring a point to secure a guaranteed place at the 2002 FIFA World Cup going into their final qualifying match against Greece, it's fair to say they didn't get off to the best start as Angelos Charisteas gave the visitors a first-half lead at Old Trafford.

Substitute Teddy Sheringham equalised in the 68th minute, heading in a David Beckham free-kick just seconds after coming on as a replacement for Robbie Fowler. But Demis Nikolaidis restored Greece's advantage moments later as he beat Nigel Martyn from close range.

In the third minute of stoppage time at the end of the game, Beckham stepped forward to take a free-kick after Sheringham had been fouled around 30 yards from the Greek goal. 'Becks' curled his effort over the wall and into the top corner of the net with unerring accuracy to seal a 2-2 draw and send England to the finals of the 2002 FIFA World Cup.

KIERAN TRIPPIER

Croatia 2-1 England (after extra-time)
2018 FIFA World Cup semi-final
July 11, 2018
Luzhniki Stadium, Moscow

Less than five minutes into England's World Cup semi-final against Croatia in 2018, the Three Lions were awarded a free-kick after Luka Modric fouled Dele Alli around 25 yards from goal.

Kieran Trippier took the kick and found the top right corner of the net with a brilliant effort with his right foot. The strike, timed at four minutes and 44 seconds, was the fastest goal scored in a World Cup semi-final since Vava netted for Brazil against France in 1958. He also became the first England player to score with a direct set-piece at the World Cup since David Beckham against Ecuador in 2006.

Alas, Trippier's textbook free-kick wasn't enough to see Gareth Southgate's side claim victory. Ivan Perišić levelled for Croatia to force extra-time before Mario Mandžukić got their winner in the added period of 30 minutes.

WHO AM I?!

Guess the identity of these England players from the following clues...

Player 1

I was born in Aylesbury in 1989. I currently play for Manchester City. My previous clubs include Chelsea, Leeds Carnegie, Arsenal, Notts County and Birmingham City. I scored six goals in six matches at the 2019 FIFA Women's World Cup.

Player 2

I am 'Player 1's' teammate at club and international level. I was appointed a Member of the Order of the British Empire (MBE) in the 2016 New Year Honours for services to football. I captained England at both the SheBelieves Cup and FIFA Women's World Cup in 2019.

Player 3

In my early club career, I spent loan spells with Leyton Orient, Millwall, Norwich City and Leicester City. I scored on my senior England debut against Lithuania in March 2015. I won the Golden Boot at the 2018 FIFA World Cup, scoring six goals in as many matches.

Player 4

I signed for Everton in 2017 – the same year I made my England debut. I previously played for my favourite boyhood club, Sunderland. At the 2019 UEFA Nations League Finals, I became the first goalkeeper to take (and score) a penalty in a competitive shootout for the Three Lions.

Player 5

I made my Lionesses' debut against the Netherlands in August 2006 and I have since won over 130 caps. I scored in England's 3-0 win over Norway at the 2019 FIFA Women's World Cup.

Player 6

I was born in Liverpool on October 7, 1998. I made my England debut in a friendly match against Costa Rica at Elland Road, Leeds in June 2018. A year later, I became a UEFA Champions League winner at the age of 20.

Player 7

Early in my career, I was loaned to Leicester City, Birmingham City, Brighton & Hove Albion and Derby County. I scored my first England goal against the Netherlands in 2018. My cousin Gabby George has played for the Lionesses.

Player 8

I used to play for my home town club, MK Dons. I was named as the PFA Young Player of the Year in both 2016 and 2017. I scored in England's 2-0 win over Sweden at the 2018 FIFA World Cup.

DEVELOPMENT TEAMS

A round-up from selected England national teams at development level

WOMEN'S U21s

Mo Marley's side enjoyed success at the U23 Open Nordic Tournament in 2019 with victories over China (3-0) and the Netherlands (4-1), as well as a goalless draw with Norway which saw them win the competition in Sweden.

MEN'S U21s

The Young Lions failed to progress past the group stage at the 2019 UEFA Under-21 Championships but Aidy Boothroyd's side could at least take some consolation from their involvement in some entertaining matches in Italy and San Marino. England led for the majority of the second half in their opening Group C fixture with France in Cesena through a stunning Phil Foden goal. Jonathan Ikoné levelled for France with just a minute of normal time remaining while a cruel own goal in the fifth-minute of stoppage time saw Boothroyd's team fall to a 2-1 defeat.

All six goals in England's match against Romania in Cesena came in the last 14 minutes of the match plus stoppage time. Strikes from Demarai Gray and

Tammy Abraham cancelled out efforts from George Pușcaș and Ianis Hagi before a brace from Florinel Coman condemned the Young Lions to a 4-2 defeat. In their final group fixture, goals from Reiss Nelson (penalty), James Maddison and Jonjoe Kenny helped Boothroyd's team to a 3-3 draw with Croatia.

England face the likes of Albania, Andorra, Austria, Kosovo and Turkey in 2020 in qualifying matches for the 2021 UEFA Under-21 Championships.

MEN'S U20s

After the disappointment of missing out on the 2019 FIFA U20 World Cup in Poland, the focus for the Young Lions will be making the 2021 tournament for which qualification takes place via the UEFA U19 Euros in 2020. England previously won the competition in 2017, beating Venezuela 1-0 in the final thanks to a goal from Dominic Calvert-Lewin.

WOMEN'S U19s

Rehanne Skinner's squad made the trip north of the border to Scotland for the 2019 U19 Euro Finals in July, after a successful season in qualifying. They suffered a narrow 2-1 defeat to Germany in their opener and then lost by 1-0 against Spain, which saw them exit the tournament at the group stage. The Young Lionesses ended on a high though, as Ebony Salmon scored a fine goal to beat Belgium in their final group match.

MEN'S U19s

England's U19 side will be hoping to make it to the UEFA Under-19 Championship in Northern Ireland in 2020 – a tournament where they triumphed in back in 2017. The Young Lions are two-time competition runners-up – in 2005 and 2009 – while they reached the semi-finals in 2010, 2012 and 2016. Qualification for the Euros starts in November, before the Elite Round stage takes place in March 2020.

MEN'S U18s

The U18s performed well in the various competitions they entered in 2019, finishing in second place at the UAE Sports Chain Cup in Dubai. The Young Lions enjoyed a 4-1 victory over Japan and beat Mexico 3-2 during the tournament but finished behind Czech Republic in the table, who won 1-0 in the head-to-head encounter between the two nations. Liverpool's Curtis Jones was named the tournament's best player.

England also made it through to the final of an eight-team tournament in Slovakia as they beat Russia and Japan and drew with the host nation in the group stage. In the final against Spain, England goalkeeper Marcus Dewhurst scored with just 30 seconds of the match remaining to cancel out Cedric Noubi's tenth minute opener. Spain eventually triumphed 4-3 on penalties.

WOMEN'S U17s

Gemma Grainger's U17s were desperately unlucky not to make it to the semi-finals of the 2019 UEFA Women's Championship, finishing third in their group despite matching the points tally of eventual finalists the Netherlands and tournament winners Germany. After a 4-0 defeat to Germany in their opening match, the Young Lionesses bounced back with a 2-1 victory over Austria thanks to goals from Lucy Johnson and Katie Robinson. Robinson and Keri Matthews were on target in a 2-0 success over the Dutch in their final group fixture. With the top three teams in the group all having accrued six points, Skinner's team were denied a place in the last four by virtue of an inferior head-to-head goal difference.

MEN'S U17s

Arsenal's Sam Greenwood scored three goals in three matches at the 2019 UEFA Under-17 Championships in the Republic of Ireland but the Young Lions were unable to progress to the knockout phase of the competition. A 1-1 draw with France in their opening Group B game was followed by a 5-2 defeat to the Netherlands. England enjoyed a 3-1 win over Sweden in their final match of the tournament thanks to strikes from Greenwood, Brighton & Hove Albion's Teddy Jenks and Joe Gelhardt of Wigan Athletic.

QUIZ AND PUZZLE ANSWERS

Page 23:
What's The Score?

a) England 4 West Germany 2

b) England 4 Netherlands 1

c) Germany 1 England 5

d) England 6 Panama 1

e) Spain 2 England 3

f) England 3 Cameroon 0

Page 40: Wordsearch

Page 43:
England Quiz

1) 1968

2) Maracanã

3) Republic of Ireland

4) David Platt

5) Paul Gascoigne

6) Spain

7) Alan Shearer

8) Wembley Stadium

9) Munich

10) Teddy Sheringham

11) Lyon

12) SheBelieves Cup

13) Nikita Parris

14) Norway

15) Liverpool

16) Marcus Rashford

17) Ben Chilwell

18) 35

19) Chelsea

20) 12

Page 40: Wordsearch

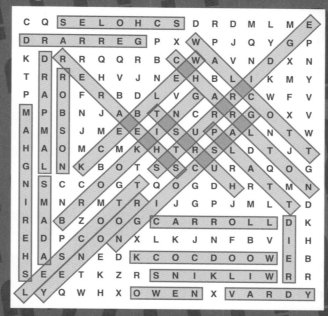

Page 50:
Who Am I?!

Player 1: Ellen White

Player 2: Steph Houghton

Player 3: Harry Kane

Player 4: Jordan Pickford

Player 5: Jill Scott

Player 6: Trent Alexander-Arnold

Player 7: Jesse Lingard

Player 8: Dele Alli

SPOT THE PLAYERS

Can you spot the six England stars hiding in the crowd?